Dedicated to Lorna Burroughs and her brilliant pupils

First Book of Treble Recorder Solos

Edited for treble (alto) recorder and piano

by

WALTER BERGMANN

Faber Music Limited
London

© 1978 by Faber Music Ltd
First published in 1978 by Faber Music Ltd
Bloomsbury House 74–77 Great Russell Street London WC1B 3DA
Music engraved by Jack Thompson
Cover design by Shirley Tucker
Printed in England by Caligraving Ltd
All rights reserved

ISBN10: 0-571-50546-5
EAN13: 978-0-571-50546-3

To buy Faber Music publications or to find out about the full range of titles available please contact your local music retailer or Faber Music sales enquiries:

Faber Music Limited, Burnt Mill, Elizabeth Way, Harlow, CM20 2HX England
Tel: +44 (0)1279 82 89 82   Fax: +44 (0)1279 82 89 83
sales@fabermusic.com   fabermusicstore.com

Contents

Preface

#	Title	Page
1	A Song	1
2	Waltz on two notes	1
3	Berceuse *(French)*	2
4	Triste	2
5	Miniature March	3
6	Waltz on three notes	3
7	Old German Christmas Song	4
8	Ländler	4
9	Scottish Air	5
10	A la claire fontaine *(French)*	5
11	The 'Passion Chorale' *(German)*	6
12	La Volta *(English)*	6
13	Les Bouffons *(French)*	7
14	Gavotte *Handel*	7
15	Minuet *Dieupart*	8
16	Polka *(Czech)*	8
17	Variations on 'Lavender's Blue'	9
18	A Christmas Song *Bach*	10
19	Babiole *Naudot*	10
20	Musette *Chédeville*	11
21	Pony Trot	12
22	Arpeggio Study	13
23	Italian Folk Song	14
24	Scherzando	14
25	Minuet *Paisible*	15
26	Andante from Partita No. 1 *Telemann*	16
27	Norwegian Call	17
28	Duet	17
29	Gavotte *Pepusch*	18
30	Hornpipe	18
31	Ballad	20
32	Chromatic	21
33	Grave *Paisible*	22
34	Waltz – Variations *Britten*	23
35	Chaconne from 'The Fairy Queen' *Purcell*	26

Preface

These pieces offer – in progressive order – an introduction to the world of music-*making* as well as to the basic technique of the treble (alto) recorder. They are expressly designed for the true beginner on the instrument; the piano accompaniments are also simple enough for a student player. Short footnotes in the recorder part offer some technical and musical advice, but much is left to the imagination of the players; in music, discovering by oneself is often more valuable, and surely more exciting, than being spoon-fed.

Charts for both standard fingering and trill (shake) fingering are included in the recorder part.

The accompanying pianist is advised to study the piano part beforehand, and to keep a balance with the recorder player, i.e. to *accompany* and not to lead.

All the pieces are edited or arranged or, if not stated otherwise, composed by me.

WALTER BERGMANN

1. A Song

2. Waltz on two notes

© 1978 by Faber Music Ltd. Unauthorised reproduction of any part of this publication is illegal.

3. Berceuse

French

4. Triste

5. Miniature March

6. Waltz on three notes

7. Old German Christmas Song

8. Ländler

9. Scottish Air

10. A la claire fontaine

French

11. The "Passion Chorale"

12. La Volta

Old English

15. Minuet
FRANCIS DIEUPART

16. Polka
Czech traditional

17. Variations on "Lavender's Blue"

18. A Christmas Song

JOHANN SEBASTIAN BACH
(1685-1750)

19. Babiole

JEAN JAQUES NAUDOT
(18th century)

20. Musette

ESPRIT-PHILIPPE CHÉDEVILLE
(1696-1762)

21. Pony Trot

Recorder part

Dedicated to Lorna Burroughs and her brilliant pupils

First Book of Treble Recorder Solos

Edited for treble (alto) recorder and piano

by

WALTER BERGMANN

Contents

1	A Song	Page 2	19	Babiole *Naudot*	7
2	Waltz on two notes	2	20	Musette *Chédeville*	8
3	Berceuse *(French)*	2	21	Pony Trot	8
4	Triste	2	22	Arpeggio Study	8
5	Miniature March	3	23	Italian Folk Song	9
6	Waltz on three notes	3	24	Scherzando	9
7	Old German Christmas Song	3	25	Minuet *Paisible*	9
8	Ländler	4	26	Andante from Partita No. 1 *Telemann*	10
9	Scottish Air	4	27	Norwegian Call	10
10	A la claire fontaine *(French)*	4	28	Duet	10
11	The 'Passion Chorale' *(German)*	4	29	Gavotte *Pepusch*	11
12	La Volta *(English)*	5	30	Hornpipe	11
13	Les Bouffons *(French)*	5	31	Ballad	12
14	Gavotte *Handel*	5	32	Chromatic	12
15	Minuet *Dieupart*	6	33	Grave *Paisible*	12
16	Polka *(Czech)*	6	34	Waltz – Variations *Britten*	13
17	Variations on 'Lavender's Blue'	6	35	Chaconne from 'The Fairy Queen' *Purcell*	14
18	A Christmas Song *Bach*	7		Fingering charts	15

All rights reserved

Faber Music Ltd · Bloomsbury House 74–77, Great Russell Street, London WC1B 3DA · All rights reserved

1. A Song

This piece requires even blowing, gentle tonguing and, where indicated, slurring.

2. Waltz on two notes

3. Berceuse

French traditional

4. Triste

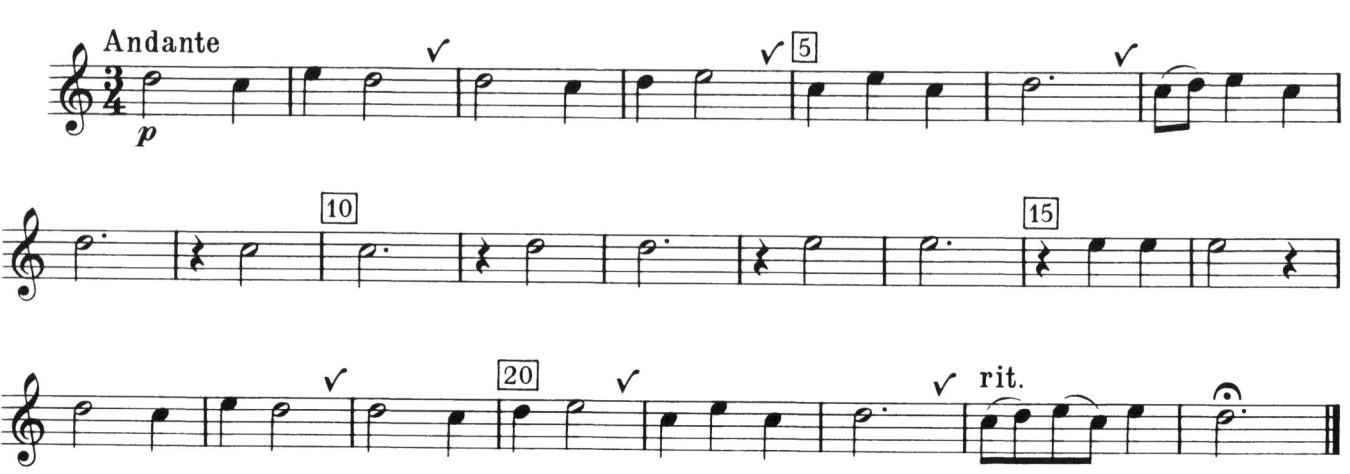

© 1978 by Faber Music Ltd.

5. Miniature March

Play all notes well detached. *f* = play loud (but not out of tune).

6. Waltz on three notes

7. Old German Christmas Song

8. Ländler

A Ländler is a (mainly Austrian) slowish dance.

9. Scottish Air

Molto sostenuto = *very* sustained; *espressivo* = with expression; *mf* = neither loud nor soft.

10. A la claire fontaine

11. The "Passion Chorale"

Originally the melody of a love madrigal by Hans Leo Hassler (1564-1612), this tune was used in the present form by the Protestant Church as a chorale (hymn) which became famous by the use which J. S. Bach made of it in his St. Matthew Passion.

12. La Volta

Old English

The Volta was a dance popular in the Elizabethan period.

13. Les Bouffons

from Arbeau's Orchésographie (1589)

Bouffons = comedians. With the piano accompaniment this piece should give a "pipe and tabor" effect.

14. Gavotte

GEORGE FREDERIC HANDEL
(1685-1759)

15. Minuet

FRANCIS DIEUPART

Dieupart came to England in the first years of the 18th century. His harpsichord suites (which he arranged himself for "violon ou flûte") were admired and copied by J. S. Bach. In 1717 Dieupart published six sonatas for the treble recorder. He died in 1740.

16. Polka

Czech traditional

17. Variations on "Lavender's Blue"

18. A Christmas Song

JOHANN SEBASTIAN BACH
(1685-1750)

19. Babiole

JEAN JAQUES NAUDOT
(18th century)

On the recorder the lower and shorter notes are weaker than the higher and longer ones. The (editorial) accents in bars 1, 2, 5, 6, 9 and 10 will admonish the player to counteract these acoustical phenomena. Babiole = bauble. Naudot composed many works for "musette" (a small French bagpipe) "or flûte à bec" (recorder) "or flûte traversière" (flute) "or oboe" etc. This is one of them.

20. Musette

ESPRIT-PHILIPPE CHÉDEVILLE
(1696-1762)

A musette was both a French bagpipe and a dance-like piece of music of pastoral character. This musette was intended for the same variety of musical instruments as Naudot's Babiole (No. 19).

21. Pony Trot

22. Arpeggio Study

23. Italian Folk Song

24. Scherzando

ten. = tenuto = (slightly) sustained; scherzando = frolicking

25. Minuet

JAMES PAISIBLE
(c. 1650-1721)

Paisible, himself a famous recorder player, was a prolific composer for his instrument.

26. Andante from Partita No. 1

GEORG PHILIPP TELEMANN
(1681-1767)

Telemann used the recorder in a great variety of works; chamber music, concertos, oratorios, operas, suites etc.
He is recognised as one of the greatest composers of the baroque era.

27. Norwegian Call

Play very slowly and as softly as possible in order to create an atmosphere of complete tranquillity.

28. Duet

29. Gavotte

JOHN CHRISTOPHER PEPUSCH
(1667-1752)

Pepusch, a German emigrant to England, is best known by his arrangement of the music for John Gay's 'Beggar's Opera' (1728). He used the recorder frequently in his numerous compositions.

30. Hornpipe

Stringendo = getting quicker

31. Ballad

32. Chromatic

Chromatic = progressing in semitones; appassionato = with passion

33. Grave

JAMES PAISIBLE

Paisible: see No. 25

34. Waltz–Variations

BENJAMIN BRITTEN
(1913-1976)

This piece was written by Benjamin Britten for the piano before he was 12, and has been arranged (by permission of the composer) for recorder and piano. Britten has composed for recorders in several works including *Noyes Fludde*, *A Midsummer Night's Dream*, and the *Alpine Suite*.

35. Chaconne
from *The Fairy Queen*

HENRY PURCELL
(1659-1695)

The chaconne rhythm | ♩ ♩. ♪ | has to be played approximately like | ♪ 𝄾 ♩. ♪ |

STANDARD FINGERING CHART

Figures indicate covered holes.
A figure with a stroke through it indicates a half-covered hole.

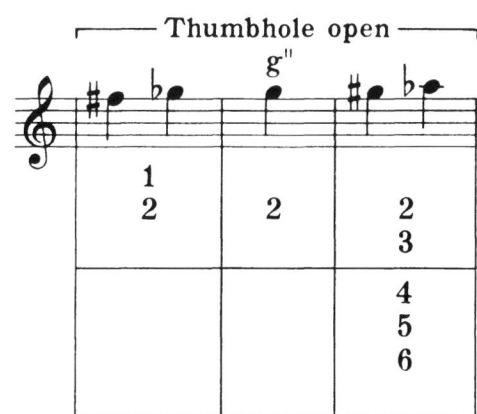

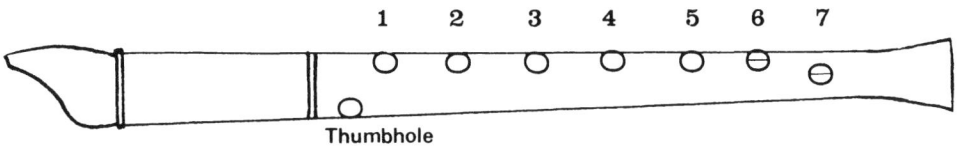

TRILL (SHAKE) FINGERING CHART

Most trills are played with the normal fingerings, but sometimes this is unduly difficult, or even impossible. This chart shows the exceptional fingerings most frequently used. As in the Standard Fingering Chart figures indicate covered holes, figures with a stroke through them indicating half-covered holes.

Thumbhole covered

1	1	1	1	1	1*tr*		1*tr*	
2	2					2		2*tr*
3		3	3	3*tr*	3	3*tr*		
4*tr*	4	4	4	4	4			
	5	5*tr*	5*tr*					
6*tr*	6*tr*	6*tr*	~~6~~		(6			
7	7*tr*	~~7~~			7)			

Thumbhole open

1	1		1	1
2	2	2	2	2
3	3	3	3	3
4	4	4	4	4
5	5*tr*	5	5*tr*	
6	6	6*tr*	6	6
7*tr*	7			7*tr*

Thumbhole partly covered

1	1	1	1	1	1
2	2	2	2	2	2
3	3*tr*		3*tr*	~~3~~*tr*	~~3~~
		4	4	4	4
5	5		5	5	5
~~6~~*tr*		6*tr*	6	6	6*tr*
			7*tr*	7*tr*	7*tr*

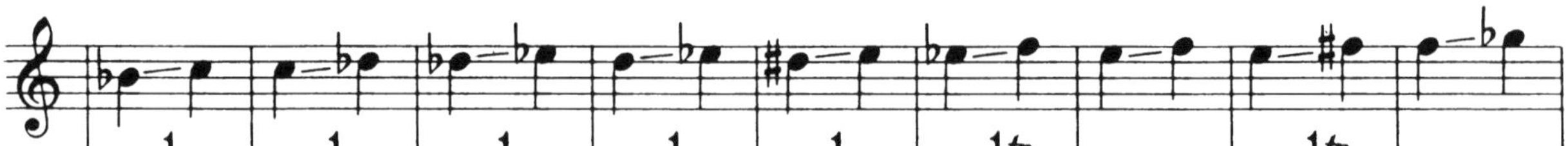

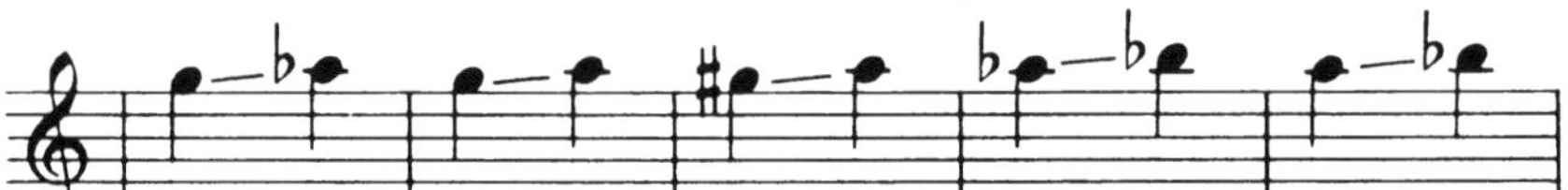

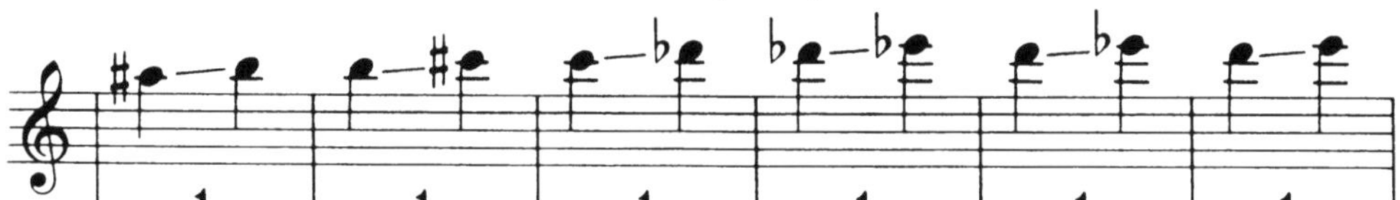

22. Arpeggio Study

23. Italian Folk Song

24. Scherzando

25. Minuet

JAMES PAISIBLE
(c. 1650-1721)

26. Andante from Partita No. 1

GEORG PHILIPP TELEMANN
(1681-1767)

27. Norwegian Call

28. Duet

29. Gavotte

JOHN CHRISTOPHER PEPUSCH
(1667-1752)

30. Hornpipe

31. Ballad

32. Chromatic

33. Grave

JAMES PAISIBLE

34. Waltz–Variations

BENJAMIN BRITTEN
(1913-1976)

35. Chaconne
from *The Fairy Queen*

HENRY PURCELL
(1659-1695)